RUSSELL WILSON
Making a Difference as a Quarterback

By Katie Kawa

PUBLISHING

People Who Make a Difference

Published in 2023 by
KidHaven Publishing, an Imprint of Greenhaven Publishing, LLC
29 E. 21st Street
New York, NY 10010

Designer: Deanna Paternostro
Editor: Katie Kawa

Photo credits: Cover, pp. 17, 18 Featureflash Photo Agency/Shutterstock.com; pp. 5, 13 Grindstone Media Group/Shutterstock.com; p. 7 Jordan Strauss/Invision/AP Images; p. 9 Lynne Sladky/ AP Images; p. 11 Abaca Press/Alamy Stock Photo; p. 15 ZUMA Press/Alamy Stock Photo; p. 20 Kathy Hutchins/Shutterstock.com; p. 21 T.Sumaetho/Shutterstock.com.

Cataloging-in-Publication Data

Names: Kawa, Katie.
Title: Russell Wilson: making a difference as a quarterback / Katie Kawa.
Description: New York : KidHaven Publishing, 2023. | Series: People who make a difference | Includes glossary and index.
Identifiers: ISBN 9781534541818 (pbk.) | ISBN 9781534541832 (library bound) | ISBN 9781534541825 (6pack) | ISBN 9781534541849 (ebook)
Subjects: LCSH: Wilson, Russell, 1988—Juvenile literature. | Seattle Seahawks (Football team)– Juvenile literature. | Quarterbacks (Football)–United States–Biography–Juvenile literature.
Classification: LCC GV939.W56 K39 2023 | DDC 796.332092 B–dc23

Printed in the United States of America

CPSIA compliance information: Batch #CSKH23: For further information contact Greenhaven Publishing LLC, New York, New York at 1-844-317-7404.

Please visit our website, www.greenhavenpublishing.com. For a free color catalog of all our high-quality books, call toll free 1-844-317-7404 or fax 1-844-317-7405.

Find us on

CONTENTS

A LEADER ON AND OFF THE FIELD

A quarterback is often seen as a leader on the football field. They make big plays, throw touchdown passes, and help their team succeed. Their leadership and ability to work with their teammates often makes a huge difference in how their team plays.

Russell Wilson has been a quarterback in the National Football League (NFL) for a decade. In that time, he's led his teammates to huge wins, including a Super Bowl victory. Russell is also known as a leader in his community too. He wants to make a difference both on and off the football field, and he works hard to make it happen.

In His Words

"If I can serve others, I think that's my **responsibility**. It's my responsibility as a quarterback to serve to help my teammates, but more importantly, it's an opportunity and gift to be able to give back to others around the country, around the world."

— **Remarks** after winning the 2020 Walter Payton NFL Man of the Year Award

Russell Wilson is one of the most famous quarterbacks in the NFL, but he knows that what he does off the field matters just as much as what he does on it. In fact, he won the 2020 Walter Payton NFL Man of the Year Award—an honor given to a player who makes a big difference off the field in their community.

A FAMILY OF ATHLETES

Russell Wilson began playing football at a young age. He was born on November 29, 1988, in Cincinnati, Ohio, but he spent most of his early life in Richmond, Virginia. Russell's dad, Harrison Wilson III, was a football and baseball player in college. Russell's brother and sister are also good at sports, and Russell learned a lot about football by playing it with his brother when they were kids.

Russell was very close to his dad. He played baseball and football just like Harrison. After Harrison died in 2010, Russell continued to share the lessons his dad taught him about sports— and about life.

In His Words

"The thing my dad used to always tell me as a young kid was, 'Son, why not you?' ... 'Why not you play pro baseball, why not you play pro football?' ... And I think that's the question we all have to ask ourselves."

— Remarks after winning the 2020 Walter Payton NFL Man of the Year Award

Russell comes from a family of athletes—people who play sports. His brother, Harry, also played baseball and football in college. His sister, Anna, who's shown with him here, has had a successful college basketball **career**.

A STAR IN TWO SPORTS

Russell was good at baseball, basketball, and football in high school. However, he chose to play only baseball and football in college at North Carolina State University. Russell was so good at baseball that he was chosen in the Major League Baseball (MLB) **draft**. He even played baseball in the **minor leagues** in 2010 and 2011.

In 2011, Russell changed schools. He played his final year of college football at the University of Wisconsin–Madison. He had a very successful year and was chosen by the Seattle Seahawks in the 2012 NFL draft. By then, Russell had chosen to **focus** on football over baseball.

In His Words

"Remember that the moments when life tells you yes aren't the ones that define you. The moments that really matter are the moments when life tells you no."

— Speech to **graduates** in 2016

Although Russell chose to focus more on football than baseball as an adult, he's still part of the MLB system. In fact, he's played in games during MLB spring training, including this one with the New York Yankees in 2018.

SUPER BOWL SUCCESS

Russell was named the starting quarterback of the Seahawks in his rookie, or first, season. He had a great rookie year and even led his team to the playoffs. The next year, Russell and the Seahawks had even more success. He led them all the way to the Super Bowl in 2014! The Seahawks beat the Denver Broncos in Super Bowl XLVIII, with a final score of 43–8.

The Seahawks didn't slow down after winning the Super Bowl. They made it back to the NFL's most important game the next year, but they lost to the New England Patriots.

In His Words

"I want to be the best player the next Sunday that I have, and that's all I know. That's the thing about this game—you have to work for everything and earn everything."

— Interview with *GQ* magazine from May 2019

Russell is shown here after winning the Super Bowl in 2014. He threw two touchdown passes to help his team win the game.

INSPIRING OTHERS

Throughout his career, Russell has continued to find success. He's known for his ability make plays by running as well as by passing. Although Russell is now part of a small group of quarterbacks who've led their teams to Super Bowl wins, people didn't always believe in him. They thought he was too short to be successful, but he proved them wrong!

Russell became the shortest quarterback to win a Super Bowl. He also became only the second Black quarterback at the time to win a Super Bowl. Russell has used his fame to call attention to problems Black people face in the United States.

In His Words

"Black lives matter. So where do we go from here? ... I see a world of hurt, pain, and despair [hopelessness]. But I also see a new **generation**, a generation that is calling out in ... need for lasting change."

– Speech to open the 2020 ESPY Awards

Russell has **inspired** many young Black athletes to follow their football dreams.

HELPING KIDS

Russell knows a lot of kids look up to him, and he tries to set a good example for them. He loves helping kids, and he works to make a difference in their lives in many ways. One of the biggest ways he does this is by visiting kids who are sick in the hospital. Russell started making weekly visits to Seattle Children's Hospital soon after he was drafted by the Seahawks.

Russell also started the Why Not You Foundation in 2014. Its goal is to help young people in areas such as education, health care, and fighting **poverty**.

In His Words

"I got out here [to Seattle] and my whole thought process on my heart was, I want to make a difference."

— Remarks after winning the 2020 Walter Payton NFL Man of the Year Award

The Why Not You Foundation got its name from the question Russell's dad used to ask him to help him believe in himself: Why not you?

FAMILY LIFE

Helping kids who are sick or in need is a big part of Russell's life, and spending time with his owns kids is also very important to him. In 2016, Russell married Ciara, who's a famous singer. He became her son Future Zahir's stepfather when they got married. Then, in 2017, Russell and Ciara celebrated the birth of their daughter, Sienna Princess. In 2020, Ciara gave birth to a son—Win Harrison.

Russell and Ciara work together to make a difference. Ciara is a big part of the Why Not You Foundation, and she and Russell have given money to support many causes they care about.

In His Words

"You can't do it alone. You've got to surround yourself with good people."

— Speech to graduates in 2016

Russell and Ciara want to be good parents to their kids while helping other young people too. They're shown here with Future and Sienna.

A SPECIAL SCHOOL

Russell and Ciara took a big step toward making life better for many kids in the Seattle, Washington, area in 2020. That's when they announced plans for Why Not You Academy—a special school to give kids the support they need to succeed after they finish their time as students.

Why Not You Academy opened in 2021. It allows students to learn through internships in which they gain skills by working in a field that interests them. The school also matches its students with advisors, or people who can give them advice and help. Russell hopes it's the first of many similar schools across the country.

In His Words

"I've always thought about others and that's always something that's been important to Ciara and me."

— Remarks after winning the 2020 Walter Payton NFL Man of the Year Award

The Life of
Russell Wilson

1988
Russell Wilson is born on November 29 in Cincinnati, Ohio.

2010
Russell's father, Harrison Wilson III, dies.

2010–2011
Russell plays baseball in the minor leagues.

2011
Russell leaves North Carolina State University and plays his final year of college football at the University of Wisconsin–Madison.

2012
Russell is drafted by the Seattle Seahawks of the NFL.

2014
The Seahawks win Super Bowl XLVIII, and Russell starts the Why Not You Foundation.

2015
The Seahawks reach the Super Bowl for the second straight year but lose to the New England Patriots.

2016
Russell marries Ciara.

2017
Sienna Princess Wilson is born.

2020
Win Harrison Wilson is born, and plans for Why Not You Academy are announced.

2021
Why Not You Academy opens, and Russell and Ciara help raise almost $3 million to help Seattle Children's Hospital.

2022
Russell begins playing for the Denver Broncos.

Russell is known not just for his skills on the football field, but also for all he's done to help people in his community.

NEW WAYS TO GIVE BACK

Russell is always looking for new ways to give back. In 2020, the **COVID-19 pandemic** hit Seattle, and Russell and Ciara wanted to help. They worked with food banks to donate, or give away, 1 million meals to families who needed food during this hard time. Then, in 2021, they helped raise almost $3 million to support Seattle Children's Hospital in the fight against childhood **cancer**.

Russell Wilson knows how to make big plays happen on the football field. However, it's the big things he does for others in his community that are even more important.

In His Words

"The one thing that's going to always get us through—not just us, but the world—at the center of all of that is love … With giving back: love at the center of it all. With our family: love at the center of it all. With society and the social **injustices**, and all of the things going on … love is at the center of it all."

— Interview with *GQ* magazine from February 2021

Be Like Russell Wilson!

Practice doing things you love—whether it's playing a sport, dancing, writing, cooking, or any other activity you enjoy.

Work hard in school.

Believe in yourself, and help the people around you believe in themselves too. Tell them why you think they can succeed!

Raise money for groups that help sick kids.

Donate money or food to food banks.

Make cards for people who are in the hospital.

If you know someone who's sick, try to cheer them up with a visit, a card, or a phone call.

If you feel comfortable, take the steps to be a leader on a sports team, in a club at school, or in student government.

You don't have to be a quarterback in the NFL to be a leader in your family or your community. These are just a few ways to get started!

GLOSSARY

cancer: A sometimes deadly sickness in which cells grow in a way they should not, often forming tumors, or growths, that harm the body.

career: A period of time spent doing a job or activity.

COVID-19 pandemic: An event that began in China in 2019 in which a disease that causes breathing problems, a fever, and other health issues spread rapidly around the world and made millions of people sick in a short period of time.

draft: An event where sports teams choose players to play for them.

focus: To direct attention or effort at something.

generation: A group of people born and living during the same time.

graduate: A person who has finished the required course of study in a school.

injustice: Unfair treatment.

inspire: To move someone to do something great.

minor leagues: A group of professional baseball teams that is below the highest level in the sport.

poverty: The state of being poor.

remark: Something that someone says.

responsibility: A duty that a person should do.

FOR MORE INFORMATION

WEBSITES

Russell Wilson: ESPN

www.espn.com/nfl/player/_/id/14881/russell-wilson

Visit this website for facts, news stories, and videos about Russell Wilson's NFL career.

Why Not You Foundation

whynotyoufdn.org

This is the official website of Russell Wilson's Why Not You Foundation, and it features links to learn more about the foundation itself and Why Not You Academy.

BOOKS

Coleman, Ted. *Russell Wilson: Superstar Quarterback*. Burnsville, MN: Press Box Books, 2020.

Fishman, Jon M. *Russell Wilson*. Minneapolis, MN: Lerner Publications, 2021.

Morey, Allan. *Superstars of the Seattle Seahawks*. Mankato, MN: Amicus, 2019.

INDEX